WORSHIP

Creating opportunities to meet and respond to God

Written by Daniel Benedict, Jr.
General Board of Discipleship

WORSHIP

Copyright © 2000 by Cokesbury

All rights reserved.
United Methodist churches and other official United Methodist bodies may reproduce up to 500 words from this publication, provided the following notice appears with the excerpted material: From *Worship: 2001–2004*. Copyright © 2000 by Cokesbury. Used by permission.

Requests for quotations exceeding 500 words should be addressed to Permissions Office, Abingdon Press, P.O. Box 801, 201 Eighth Avenue South, Nashville, TN 37202-0801.

This book is printed on elemental-chlorine–free paper.

ISBN 0-687-03528-7

All scripture quotations unless noted otherwise are taken from the *New Revised Standard Version of the Bible,* copyrighted 1989, Division of Christian Education of the National Council of the Churches of Christ in the United States of America. Used by permission. All rights reserved.

MANUFACTURED IN THE UNITED STATES OF AMERICA

CONTENTS

4/Our Identity, Call, and Mission
6/Getting Started
    6/What's My Job?
    6/What Are My Basic Responsibilities?
    7/What Does the Chairperson Do?
    7/Quick Start Tips

8/Help Is Available

9/First, Pray and Listen

10/Second, Think About:
    10/What Makes Worship Vital?
    11/Why Does Vitality in Worship Matter?
    12/What Vision Moves You?

13/What Can You Do to Lead Toward Vital Worship?
    13/Stay in Communication with the Pastor
    13/Guide the Worship Ministry Group
    17/Plan Worship
    19/Work with the Music Leader(s)
    21/Promote the Spiritual Life of Your Congregation
    23/Participate in the Church Council and Charge Conference
    25/Discover Worship Resources
    25/Participate in Training Events
    25/More Paths to Vital Worship

28/A Worksheet for Planning a Worship Service

29/Resources

Daniel T. Benedict serves as Worship Resources Director for The General Board of Discipleship of The United Methodist Church. A writer, teacher, and liturgy specialist, he co-authored *Contemporary Worship for the 21st Century* and authored *Come to the Waters*. He is an ordained elder in the California Pacific Annual Conference and served as a pastor of churches in New York and California before taking his current position.

Dan's passion is for crafting liturgy and presiding in worship. He is married and father of two grown children. In leisure time he enjoys retreats, gardening, walking, cooking, and surfing the Internet.

Our Identity, Call, and Mission

About now a small voice in the back of your mind may be whispering, "What am I doing here? To what have I said yes? What is my role?" At the same time you may be aware that your congregation has extended to you a *call—a call to serve*. And you have said *yes—yes to leading in a vital mission*.

The mission of The United Methodist Church is to make disciples of Jesus Christ. You have agreed to serve as a leader bringing your unique passions, gifts, and abilities to the church. When the leaders focus on the church's purpose—*its mission of making disciples of Jesus Christ*—and link that purpose to the passions of the people, amazing things can happen.

The fundamental way we fulfill our mission is to reach out to people in the name of Jesus Christ, to relate people to God, to nurture and strengthen them in their journey of discipleship, and to send them into the world to be the church—inviting and receiving others in the name of Jesus Christ. We call this the primary task of The United Methodist Church. Effective leaders keep the whole of the primary task in their sight, working to keep all of its aspects in concert.

Leaders in the church must be first, and foremost, spiritual leaders who model and embrace Christian discipline and teaching. *By practicing the means of grace*—prayer, fasting, studying Scripture, corporate worship, celebration of the Lord's Supper, Christian conversation, and acts of mercy—*church leaders stay tuned to the mission of the church and live out the primary task.* Members and would-be members should be able to look to a congregation's leaders for spiritual example and direction, because true leaders are known by their fruits. People's lives are changed through their influence.

Leaders use their gifts and talents to enable others to use their gifts and talents to the fullest potential. The flow of information, inspiration, guidance, and vision from leaders is an encouragement to others on their spiritual journey. Leaders help others to see new possibilities. When leaders are focused on the mission of the church, community is built and ministry occurs. The church focused on God is alive with creative energy aimed at transformation.

Four Essential Leadership Functions

Church leaders support and strengthen the church when they pay attention to these leadership functions: (1) help people discover the current *reality in which they live; (2) bring together the congregation's understandings of <u>current</u> reality and <u>desired</u> reality into a shared vision; (3) develop the plans to help the community move from current reality toward the reality of its shared vision; and finally, (4) monitor the whole work of the church as the congregation moves with God's guidance toward its vision.*

1. Discovering Current Reality

Accurately describing current reality—the way things are—may be the most important function of leadership. The booklets in this Guideline series offer suggestions for leaders to pay attention to the various committees of the church's ministry. In addition, it is critical for church leaders—lay and clergy—to spend time together discussing the ministry of the <u>whole</u> congregation. The conversation needs to include attentiveness to God's guidance and everything that describes a congregation's "what we are, here and now." Because God is always doing a new thing, this job is continuous. When we pay attention to change, we provide a base of integrity and strength from which to move into the future. Faith in Jesus Christ and a spiritual centering in God offers the strongest foundation to move people fearlessly through the massive changes of the twenty-first century.

2. Naming Shared Vision

Ask the question, "What do you want more than anything else in the world?" and most persons will give a response that indicates that they want to live in a world filled with love, faith, security, and meaning. Because persons desire a positive future, they are willing to invest themselves in organizations that are committed to it. By its very nature, the church is devoted to the creation of a better future. When the church promises to move people personally and corporately toward their desired reality, people will invest time, energy, and resources into the church. As people see their own desires linked to the congregational vision and deeper understanding of God's future, they deepen their commitment and involvement. Building this link is a vital role of leadership.

Naming a shared vision is accomplished by asking people about their lives and their faith, and listening very carefully. By listening, we mean deep listening—the kind that requires setting aside our own agendas and entering into the worldviews of others, and listening for God through the conversation. It is a significant shift in our understanding of leadership in the church to move from telling people what we think they need to know to listening to people in order to find out who they are and what their desired realities are. Effective spiritual leaders listen to the hearts of people and begin to articulate a shared vision.

3. Developing Bridges

To span the gulf between our current reality and the hope expressed in the shared vision, leaders must build a bridge. The third critical function of leadership is to plan actions and develop systems that create the bridge across this gulf. Leaders who are elected to administrative and program committees are responsible for the ongoing work of the church and must pay attention to the present. At the same time, leaders *must* be focused on the future—keeping today and tomorrow in tension—ensuring that the church doesn't get stuck in the past, present, or future.

Church leaders who are attentive to God's leading and who can hold the tension between today and tomorrow are *visionary leaders*. Visionary leaders see it all—current reality, desired reality, and the bridges to get from one to the other.

4. Monitoring the Journey

Perhaps the most critical task for leaders is keeping an eye on the whole of the faith journey of the congregation. When leaders are constantly caught up in "doing" the administrative and program work of the church, there is not any time left for "being" with God in prayer to discern the leading of the Spirit for the congregation. Leaders must step back from "doing" constant activities in order to pay attention to the total direction of the church's mission and ministry. All elected and appointed leaders must spend time together listening to God in prayer, Bible study, conversation, and other means of grace in order to lead the entire community in the work of Christ. Anything less is not Christian spiritual leadership.

Getting Started

What's My Job?

You work with your pastor and music leader(s) to ensure that your congregation provides opportunities for worship that will help the congregation experience its relationship with God and will help it live more faithfully as a Christian community. You will work closely with the church council to respond to God's call. In short, your job is to help your church offer settings for vital worship.

What Are My Basic Responsibilities?

1. To learn about worship and about people in your congregation and community so you can plan worship appropriate to their needs.
2. To collaborate with the pastor and music leaders in planning worship.
3. To develop and support effective musical leadership in the church.

4. To promote and foster regular individual and family spiritual formation.
5. To consider other opportunities for strengthening worship (see pp. 25–27).

What Does the Chairperson Do?
You will find more detail on each of these on pages 13–25.
1. Stay in communication with the pastor and music leader(s).
2. Guide the work of the worship ministry group through the year, and if there is a worship committee (work area), plan its agendas and preside at its meetings.
3. Plan worship (at least quarterly) with the pastor, music leader(s), and others who may be responsible for planning and leading worship. This cooperative planning, led by the pastor, should outline all worship services, including scriptures, music, and any special services.
4. Consult with and support the music leader(s) in your congregation.
5. Promote the spiritual life of your congregation and all of its members.
6. Participate, if appropriate to your congregation's structure, in the church council (council on ministries and administrative board) and charge conference representing the concerns of worship.
7. Discover the literature and other resources available that are related to worship, and share with other worship leaders.
8. Participate in training events that are related to worship.

Quick Start Tips
1. **Meet with the pastor** to discover her or his concerns about worship. Discover how you can best collaborate in improving worship that strengthens congregational life and faithful discipleship.
2. **Talk with the person who previously served** in the position you now hold. Ask: "What is important for me to know as I begin to lead? Are there plans that I need to carry out?"
3. **Convene a meeting of the worship ministry committee** (if organized) or meet with other key people with worship-related responsibilities to evaluate and plan for the year. Meet within thirty days of beginning of the calendar year. Talk about mutual expectations, hopes, and values related to your congregation and its worship opportunities. Discuss and decide what your group/committee will do in the coming year. Decide how often to meet and set the dates for the year.
4. **Plan the agenda for the coming meetings.** Look at the calendar in light of seasons and special services (Advent, Lent, Christmas, Easter), and decide how far in advance you and others will need to plan.
5. **Consider the worship hopes and concerns** of people in your congregation and community. Ask questions. Listen.
6. **Explore and become familiar with the primary worship books** and

resources used in your congregation. Know the hymnal and book of worship, especially the opening sections on the basic pattern and related orders.
7. **Evaluate your congregation's worship.** What is working well? How could it be improved? Is worship in your church grounded in the best of the Christian tradition? Is it relevant to the culture and setting of your people and the community?
8. **Talk with people who have (or have had) responsibilities similar to yours.** They may be in your congregation or in other congregations.
9. **Participate in training events.** Ask your pastor, district superintendent, and/or conference program staff what events they know about.

> You are being asked to see the whole experience of worship. You are being asked to help the pastor and the musicians to hear what the congregation is saying and feeling.

Help Is Available

Know that you are not alone in your work. You have powerful allies and terrific supporters:

- The Spirit will work in you as you use the spiritual disciplines: prayer, scripture reflection, worship, and sharing with other Christians
- The pastor
- The musician(s)
- The person who served in your role before you
- Your district or annual conference's elected worship person
- Your annual conference program staff
- The worship staff of the General Board of Discipleship
- A feast of good books, magazines, Web sites, seminars, workshops, and videotapes
- Organizations committed to strengthening worship, such as the Fellowship of United Methodists in Music and Worship Arts and the Order of Saint Luke.

You will find more information about the last three bulleted items in the "Resources" at the end of this booklet. The main thing to realize is that you have ready support and assistance. The next move is yours: ASK, SEEK, KNOCK! (Matthew 7:7-11).

But before you zip off to do, let's take a little time to get a picture of worship in your church—not just how it is, but how it could be by the power of the Spirit. Then we will get to doing the things that will move toward making that picture a reality.

First, Pray and Listen

Prayer and listening are basic components of spiritual leadership. Let's experience prayer as listening. Set aside some time to listen to God. If now is not the time, choose a time and place when you can be comfortable and at ease. Pour some tea or coffee. Have pen and paper available. Relax and close your eyes, breathing deeply and exhaling a few times. *Think of a favorite place of peace and rest, and imagine being in that place.* Give yourself time to "be" in that place.

Next, recall a time when you experienced worship and the presence of God. Maybe it was a long time ago. Maybe it was in a recent service.

Take a few minutes to reenter that experience. When you are ready, thank God for that time and for what you sensed of God's love, nearness, power, grace, mercy, and call.

> Worship is not so much about us as it is about God.

When you are ready to move on, *recall what you remember about how others experienced that moment.* Maybe they experienced what you did. Maybe most missed what you experienced. Either way it is all right. List in your thoughts or on paper the factors that made the moment a deep and powerful experience for you (and others if they, too, felt the power of that moment).

Next, recall the result or impact of that moment in your life. Did you see something differently and gain insight? Did you make a commitment to do something you sensed God asking you to do? Was something consoled that was aching, or was something made whole that was broken? Did something that was angry or resentful become peaceful and centered?

Now, take time to ask: "Lord, what are my deepest longings for others who participate in worship in our church?" (You probably need to start with that question so your longings can move out of the way in listening to God and others.) Next, ask, "God, what is it that you want people to do and experience in worship? What is my pastor's vision for worship? What is the vision of the music leader(s)? What do the people long for?" Imagine people who live in the community around your church building. What do they long for in relationship to God? How could worship say to them, "You are welcome to be here and to come as you are with whatever longings and questions you have"? Listen to what you sense coming back toward you as you ask these questions. Attend to what God is saying to you.

When you are ready to break from this inward journey, thank God for this time, and hear God's blessing on you and an invitation to come and listen again. Then as a way of exiting from the inward space, say the Lord's Prayer aloud softly.

This exercise in prayer and listening is a way of beginning to shape your vision for worship in your congregation. What you now see is not all there is to see, but it gives you a place to stand in conversations that you have with other leaders. You are not a cipher without a clue; *you are a person who shares in the "great congregation" and who has a history and experience before the Holy One of Israel.*

Second, Think About

1. What Makes Worship Vital?

The worship services of your congregation are meant to be alive and vital with God's presence and the people's participation—God calling, the people responding. When worship is alive, *you know it*! When it is not, *you know that too.*

Vital or lifeless? Full or empty? *What* makes the difference? *Who* in your church can help make the difference? The following pages are designed to assist you in planning vital worship in your congregation. You are one of the many people who participate in making worship what it is and *what it can be.*

Whether your congregation is large or small, rural, small town, or big city, you know when worship is vital. There is energy in what happens. The power of God's Word touches the hurts and awakens the hopes of real people. Visitors are glad they came. People participate because the singing, the hearing, the praying, the sharing at the table, and the sending people out are done in ways that say: "This matters." In vital worship the people are addressed, touched, washed, fed, anointed, and helped in relationship to God and to one another.

In the following pages you will find invitations for conversation and reflection about worship. You may not want to read from cover to cover; maybe you will find yourself going to the places that seem to address what you really want to know now. Feel free to skip around and come back to things as you need them. *The main thing is you discover a passion for helping worship become more faithful and vital in your congregation and you sense you are a leader equipped with resources.* You are a member of the team with a unique job to do.

What Does Vital Worship Look, Feel, Smell, Taste, and Sound Like?
- People are welcomed, honored, and cared for.
- God's story/our story is always told.
- Jesus crucified and risen is proclaimed.
- Jesus is experienced as present in love and power.
- The people and the community are changed by the power of the Holy Spirit.
- People are active in singing, praying, responding.
- There is passion in the singing, preaching, and praying.
- Varied ages and cultures are welcomed.
- Things (food, water, candles, furnishings, fabrics, vessels) are used generously to point to the presence of God.
- Actions (people being baptized, greeting one another, sharing bread and cup) point to the presence of the risen Lord.
- Worship space is arranged so the people can be together and see one another.
- There are calls and responses: people experience God calling, and they respond.
- Leaders work in concert to prompt the participation of all the people.
- Leaders are prepared and expectant of God's action.
- Leaders act with the people.
- Everyone acts in ways that say, "Worship matters."
- People who are experiencing hurt and isolation receive a healing touch.
- People's hope is awakened.
- All the people have a sense of belonging and know how to participate.
- People are free to observe when they need to watch and listen as a way of preparing to participate more fully.
- There is energy, and the way worship unfolds makes sense.
- The worship reveals the planning, gifts, and preparation of the people.

You may think of others. What are they?

2. Why Does Vitality in Worship Matter?

We are living in an age of seekers.

Worship matters because people are seeking God. Perhaps the searching is more evident in people outside the church than inside it. Browse the best sellers that people are reading. Look at the growing number of twelve-step groups and New Age religious expressions. People are searching for something real, spiritual, and powerful. People are longing for meaning, belonging, and something or someone to live for.

With other leaders in your congregation, ask:
- Who are we?
- How do we enact our search for God? How does worship invite us to express the longings we have?
- How are our people searching? Are our people willing to welcome others who are searching to be active participants in worship?
- Where in worship are we most alive to God and to one another? How could we improve?

Who Is Worship For?

These questions might sound as if we are saying that worship is for people who are not now part of your church. You may be uncomfortable with that. You may be thinking, "But isn't worship for God? Isn't it about offering ourselves to God in praise and thanksgiving, in attentiveness to the gospel story told and enacted in the Scripture and sacrament?" If so, you are on target in the fuller picture concerning worship. Keep this Godward focus in view. Or you may be thinking, "Isn't worship for the people who already belong to the church? Shouldn't we start with them?" If so, you recognize that a particular community of people offers worship to God. Worship is never generic or a commodity to be consumed. Its context is always a particular group of believers.

For the moment, think of it this way: If the congregation's essential work is to do everything in such a way that people are welcomed, changed by God's story and presence, and sent out to love and serve in daily life, then worship is for all people. Worship is for everyone who longs for God—believers and seekers.

Christian worship is our public work as Christians. The door needs to be open—*wide open*—so that all people will know they are welcome to explore and search and discover the good news in Jesus Christ.

Who Are the People Not Now Part of Your Worship?
- Children
- Youth
- Baby boomers, generation X, millennials
- People of a racial/ethnic group different from most of your congregation
- People with mental or physical disabilities

Can you identify others?

3. What Vision Moves You?

Vital worship is part of the flow of people *gathering to celebrate* the good news and then *scattering to live* the good news in everyday relationships.

When worship is not vital, that flow becomes constricted like a plugged pipe. When music is lifeless or preaching is irrelevant to people's yearnings and struggles, the risen Christ seems less with us. When baptism and Communion are mere ceremonies instead of powerful moments of connection with the living Lord and one another, worship wilts.

You may be wondering, "Is lively, flowing worship about hand clapping and shouting 'Alleluia'? Is it stained glass, silence, and pipe organs?" The style and structure of vital worship can take many forms. As you lead in the search for vital worship in your setting, you will discover the uniqueness of how your congregation tells and celebrates the Christian story.

What Can You Do to Lead Toward Vital Worship?

1. Stay in Communication with the Pastor

The pastor and musicians lead worship from week to week. In some churches there is a team of persons who meet every week to plan worship for the coming Sunday and for the services several weeks from that point. In any case, you will need to get in step with these planners and gain a sense of the rhythms and patterns of their work, the decisions they make, and the way they conceive worship Sunday by Sunday and season by season. No two pastors plan the same way. Similarly, no two music leaders prepare the same way. As a first step, invite them to show you how they go about it.

Once you have a sense of their planning approach, ask if there is a way that you could support them, and find the ways in which they are open to additional minds and hands sharing the work of preparing for worship.

Then develop your own patterns for planning and preparation. Maybe you will meet monthly with the pastor to check in and see if she has any thoughts on how it's going. Maybe you will make a point to affirm the music ministry each Sunday and ask if there is anything you can do to support the work of the choir or the accompanist. Sometimes, you will lead by listening. If you sense there is an openness to talk, find the time and place.

2. Guide the Worship Ministry Group

You are responsible for guiding the work of the congregation with respect to worship. You don't manage the day-to-day affairs of worship. Others do that, but you represent the members' interests and their concerns to the pastor and staff, and you are knowledgeable about the ways the pastor and staff do the work entrusted to them.

You call the meetings of the staff and the worship team (leader of ushers, acolyte leader, greeter coordinator, and some people from the congregation who are interested or called to care about worship, though they may not have a particular worship-related task). You plan the agenda in consultation with the pastor and other worship staff. You consider the needs and expressions of the people in setting the agenda.

> Worship is not what the pastor and staff do; rather, it is the work of the people who offer themselves "in praise and thanksgiving as a holy and living sacrifice, in union with Christ's offering for us."

You also plan the agenda, keeping in mind that worship is not what the pastor and staff do; rather, it is the work of the people who offer themselves "in praise and thanksgiving as a holy and living sacrifice, in union with Christ's offering for us." (See "The Great Thanksgiving" on p. 13 of *The United Methodist Hymnal*.) Sometimes your work will be to ensure that the conversation of the meeting will focus on the work of the people as primary, while the work of the pastor and musicians is to preside and guide the people's work.

> **Here are some examples of worship meeting agendas.** You will have to adapt them to the needs and realities of your congregation. If your congregation is large and its worship life complex, you may need to meet more often.

> **Winter Worship Meeting** (Have Bibles and hymnals for each person.)
> • Scripture reflection and prayer (scripture reflection on Luke 19:29-39). Read the text twice, asking after the first time, "What word or image stands out for you?" After the second time, ask, "What invitation is here for us as a worshiping community?" Allow for silence after asking the questions. Close with prayer, perhaps using one of the prayers in the hymnal. See hymnal index 934-54.
> • Reflection on worship experience. Discuss, "What is going well? What needs to be improved?"
> • Long-range planning.
>   Here bring up or report on any long-range changes contemplated, such as redesign of the chancel space, frequency of Communion, adding a service, training acolytes, readers, and Communion servers, and so on.

- Seasonal planning for Lent and Easter. (Pass out copies of *The United Methodist Book of Worship* with book markers inserted at pp. 224, 320, and 368. You can use these as tools for orientation and reflection. You or the pastor could highlight the seasons of Lent and Easter—roughly the months of February to May.)
  Pastor shares his or her direction in preaching and worship for the approaching season. Musicians may also want to share plans. (Invite them to prepare for this ahead of time.)
  What special services will we schedule? Ash Wednesday? Holy Thursday? Good Friday? Easter Vigil? Baptism? Confirmation? What changes do we want to make in Lenten and Easter worship this year?
  What special tasks need to be assigned? To whom? How will we make special services known in the church and community?
- Short-range planning.
  Is it time for the piano to be tuned? Are readers scheduled for the next three months? Are some supplies needed? Why are we having so many problems with the sound system?

Spring Worship Meeting (Have Bibles and hymnals for each person.)
- Scripture reflection and prayer (scripture reflection on Luke 24:13-35). Read the text twice, asking after the first time, "What word or image stands out for you?" After the second time, ask, "What invitation is here for us as a worshiping community?" Close with prayer, perhaps using one of the prayers in the hymnal. See index 934-54.
- Reflection on worship experience. Discuss, "What is going well? What needs to be improved?"
- Long-range planning (see Winter meeting agenda).
- Seasonal planning for the Great Fifty Days, Trinity Sunday, and the early months of Ordinary Time. (Pass out copies of *The United Methodist Book of Worship* with book markers inserted at pp. 224 and 409. You can use these as tools for orientation and reflection. You or the pastor could highlight the Great Fifty Days, Pentecost, and Ordinary Time—roughly the months of April to August.) Pastor shares his or her direction in preaching and worship for the approaching period of time. Musicians may also want to share plans. (Invite them to prepare for this ahead of time.)
  What special services will we schedule? Will we make any changes for summer?
  What special tasks need to be assigned? To whom?
- Short-range planning. Are readers scheduled for the next three

Worship

months? Are some supplies needed? How are our hospitality and welcome? Is our publicity of service time accurate? Is our newspaper ad inviting?

Summer Worship Meeting (Have Bibles and hymnals for each person.)
- Scripture reflection and prayer. Sing "Majesty" or "Holy, Holy, Holy" or another hymn of high praise and adoration before reading Revelation 4:1-11. Read the text twice, asking after the first time, "What word or image stands out for you?" After the second time, ask, "What invitation is here for us as a worshiping community?" Close with prayer, perhaps using one of the prayers in the hymnal. See index 934-54.
- Reflection on worship experience. Discuss, "What is going well? What needs to be improved?"
- Long-range planning (see Winter agenda).
- Seasonal planning for the latter part of Ordinary Time. (Pass out copies of *The United Methodist Book of Worship* with book markers inserted at pp. 224 and 409. You can use these as tools for orientation and reflection. You or the pastor could highlight the scriptures and themes of the latter part of Ordinary Time—roughly September through November.)
Pastor shares his or her direction in preaching and worship for the approaching period of time. Musicians may also want to share plans. (Invite them to prepare for this ahead of time.)
What special services will we schedule? Will we make any changes for summer?
What special tasks need to be assigned? To whom?
- Short-range planning.

Fall Worship Meeting (Have Bibles and hymnals for each person.)
- Scripture reflection and prayer (scripture reflection on Isaiah 2:1-4). Read the text twice, asking after the first time, "What word or image stands out for you?" After the second time, ask, "What invitation is here for us as a worshiping community?" Close with prayer, perhaps using one of the prayers in the hymnal. See index 934-54.
- Reflection on worship experience. Discuss, "What is going well? What needs to be improved?"
- Long-range planning (see Winter agenda).
- Seasonal planning for the final weeks of Ordinary Time, Thanksgiving, Christ the King, Advent, and Christmas. (Pass out copies of *The United*

> *Methodist Book of Worship* with book markers inserted at pp. 224, 238, 269, and 409. You can use these as tools for orientation and reflection. You or the pastor could highlight the final weeks of Ordinary Time, Thanksgiving, Christ the King, Advent, and Christmas.)
> Pastor shares his or her direction in preaching and worship for the approaching period of time. Musicians may also want to share plans. (Invite them to prepare for this ahead of time.)
> What special services will we schedule? What special tasks need to be assigned? To whom?
> - Short-range planning. Are acolytes, readers, ushers, greeters, and communion servers scheduled?

3. Plan Worship (at Least Quarterly) with the Pastor and Others Who Are Responsible for Worship

This cooperative planning, led by the pastor, should outline all worship services, including scriptures, music, and any special services.

You may think that was discussed in 2 above. That was the "big picture" planning. *This is about detailed planning for every service.* Although your worship planners may not use a chart such as "A Worksheet for Planning a Worship Service" (p. 28), it gives you some idea of the kind of detail that needs to be planned for each service. Feel free to copy or adapt the chart to your congregation's weekly planning needs. Keep a notebook with a planning page for every service for the year in it, and fill it in as you go.

There is no single way to plan worship, but many churches are discovering that cooperative worship planning is more satisfying over time than "flying solo" planning. The way in which you and other leaders become part of cooperative worship planning will vary, depending on the size, location, traditions, and leadership patterns in your local congregation. Here are several ways planning currently takes place in churches.

Try using a planning guide to measure where you are now and to periodically measure your improvement. The main thing here is to discover how much more alive worship can become when you plan together.

One further note: weddings and funerals are occasions for a different kind of team planning. The individuals or families involved can be seen as part of a team with the pastor and church musician. They bring important knowledge and feelings to the planning work leading to the wedding or funeral.

Look for ways to plan together, trusting that you will find enjoyment and creativity in the process. Which of the following four models represents the way your congregation's worship planning is done currently? If you are not sure, explore that question with your pastor. Talk together about how you could expand and improve your cooperative worship planning capacity. Is quarterly planning frequent enough? Monthly? Weekly?

- *The Dot Approach:* Pastor J. decides on the scripture passages and title for next Sunday's sermon and lists the hymns and prayers for the bulletin. (This is often done in very small churches or in settings without an active worship area or professional music leader.)
- *The Line Approach:* Pastor K. sets out the texts and themes for the sermons several weeks or months ahead and passes them along to Musician L. and/or Secretary M. to "fill in the blanks" for the rest of the service. (This can happen where the preacher does the planning for several months ahead, focusing on sermon more than on the rest of the worship service.)
- *The Circle Approach:* Pastor N., Worship Chair O., and Music Leader P. have a meeting to consider the focus, text, and flow of a particular worship service with the aid of Bible study, dialogue, and sharing of mutual gifts. (This process can involve both lay and clergy in a regularly scheduled meeting.)
- *The Spiral Approach:* After nearly a year of working together regularly, the worship team of four to six colleagues in Christ United Methodist Church has begun to create new ways of worship and to expand the effectiveness and enjoyment of worship planning. (This process develops with the help of a growing climate of trust and an openness to the gifts of diverse persons and resources.)

Improving Worship: The Quality Questions

Your church may be frightened of change. You may be frightened of change. Maybe you remember times when someone tried to change the worship, and frustration, unhappiness, and anger resulted. Of course! Worship is important. The symbols and values of our lives are at stake!

There is another way. *People who agree to work and plan together can ask some very basic questions that we call the "quality questions."*

- *What went well today?*
- *What could be improved?*
- *What did we learn?*

Imagine your worship leaders getting together every week to ask those questions. Each might have different answers to each question. That is okay.

List all the answers. Some might be the same for one or more of you. That means you have some shared sense of what worked well or of what could be improved. Maybe you will discover that a hymn new to the congregation seems to drain the energy from the service. Does that mean you should not try new hymns or songs? Or does it mean your team needs to try some better ways to discover a new hymn or song?

The quality improvement questions let you and others make gradual but continuous improvement in your congregation's worship.

4. Work with the Music Leader(s)

We've been called the "Singing Methodists" because from the early days of the Methodist movement, song has been a primary way of celebrating and proclaiming our faith and offering our prayer.

Music accounts for at least 40 percent of the impact of a worship service. The pastor of one of the fastest growing United Methodist congregations, when asked for his "secret," said, "First music, then preaching, in that order." The music in your worship service may determine whether visitors return to your church and whether or not members feel that they have participated and been nurtured. Whether your congregation cherishes traditional sacred music "classics," rocks to contemporary praise and worship choruses, or enjoys a variety of musical styles, *the quality and content of the music in worship will in large measure determine the vitality of the overall experience of people.*

The musical players are the congregation, perhaps a director of music, the choir(s), accompanist(s), vocal and instrumental soloists, the pastor, and you. *Yours is a crucial role because you are called to see the whole picture and consult and collaborate with the leaders in ways that music and music leaders maximize their contribution to the praise of God and the response of the people.*

Here are some of your responsibilities in consulting with and supporting music leaders:
- Recognize, encourage, and nurture musicians in your congregation, both volunteer and paid.
- Work with musicians, pastor, and your pastor/staff-parish relations committee to establish clear job descriptions.
- Work with the musicians and pastor in preparing a clear vision and mission statement for your church's music ministry. Be sure that it reflects a shared understanding of music and worship in fulfilling the primary task of the church and its vision for the future.

- Develop with the musicians and pastor an intentional plan for teaching persons of all ages our heritage in song and the joy of congregational singing.
- See that an adequate budget for music is a priority for the congregation, including appropriate compensation for paid musicians, provisions for new music and instruments, their upkeep, continuing education funds, and funding for special seasonal needs.
- Develop a long-range process for discovering and training persons in your congregation and community who can become tomorrow's church musicians.

Copyright and Licensing Information

In a media-oriented age with photocopiers, VCRs, LCD projectors, and other high-tech equipment, more and more churches are finding ways to use music and video in the context of worship. There are serious ethical and legal questions involved in this use. *You need to be aware of these issues and encourage other leaders to use legal means in employing music and video with copyright restrictions.*

Music

The Copyright Act of 1976 prohibits the unauthorized reproduction of copyrighted materials including song sheets, overhead transparencies, bulletin inserts, slides, and LCD (liquid crystal display) projection. **Churches are not exempt from this law.** Permission to use some copyrighted material may be secured from organizations that have received licensing rights from various music publishers. These services allow congregations who subscribe the right to reprint texts and music (in the form of song sheets, bulletin inserts, transparencies, LCD projection, and/or slides) from a variety of, but not all, publishers. Fees are based on average worship attendance. Some record keeping is required.

- Christian Copyright Licensing, Inc. (CCLI)
6130 NE Seventy-eighth Court, Suite C11
Portland, Oregon 97218-2853
Telephone: 800-234-2446
CCLI includes the largest selection of publishers: all UM publishing groups, Word, Hope, Maranatha!, Integrity Hosanna, and others. Most praise choruses are covered by a CCLI license.

- LicenSing
Logos Production
P.O. Box 240
South St. Paul, Minnesota 55075-0240
Telephone: 800-328-0200

LicenSing covers a smaller list of publishers and is designed more for mainline, liturgical congregations. It includes all UM publishing groups, more international companies, and overlaps some of the same material covered by CCLI.

• G.I.A. Publications, Inc.
7404 South Mason Avenue
Chicago, Illinois 60638-9927
Telephone: 708-496-3800
Order line: 800-442-1358
Web site: www.giamusic.com
This company provides a wide range of music resources including music from Taizé, Iona, scripture, and liturgical songs. G.I.A. licenses churches to use its music resources under specific regulations.

Movies and Videos
Similar copyright restrictions apply to video formats of films. The opening words of commercial videos indicate that the tape is intended for "home use only." Legally, **this excludes use in churches, either for worship or for educational and entertainment settings, such as youth fellowship.** As with the music licensing companies, you may purchase a license that will allow you to legally show videos of popular films in your church. The license will allow you to show a video in its entirety, or scenes from a video, but not to edit it in any way. Modest fees are based on the anticipated viewing audience.
• Motion Picture Licensing Corporation
Harold Bower
58 Jeremiah Road
Sandy Hook, Connecticut 06482
Telephone: 800-515-8855

5. Promote the Spiritual Life of Your Congregation and All of Its Members

Our Methodist heritage is strongly oriented to the means of grace (prayer, Holy Communion, scripture and devotional reading, participation in public worship, preaching, fasting, and so on). In your church there may be specific persons, including the pastor, who focus their attention on forming habits that deepen discipleship in all of the people. Whether or not that is true in your situation, your attention to worship is clearly linked to that concern. Through your worship working group and church council, promote the spiritual life using these resources and actions.

- *Celebrate God's story every week using the lectionary and the Christian calendar.* Good worship forms faith by rehearsing God's story. The calendar and lectionary aim at making and forming Christians.
- *See and affirm the connections between worship and everyday life.* People long for the affirmation that their lives matter and that God is at work in their jobs, family life, leisure activities, friendships, and community involvement. In sermons, worship, and small groups, affirm the connections between faith and life. *Worship and Daily Life,* a book for worship planners that includes resources for affirming ministry in daily life, is available from Discipleship Resources.
- *Invite the people to read the scriptures for worship during the week.* Publish the Sunday readings in advance, and encourage all the people to read and reflect on them during the week. In this way all of the people become partners in preaching and prepared participants in the worship service.
- *Offer small groups for prayer, Bible study, and mutual accountability for discipleship.* Christian faith is not a go-it-alone experience. A basic ingredient of effective discipleship is participation in small groups where people can experience what John Wesley described as "watching over each other in love." Growing churches offer a variety of small groups.
- *Provide and encourage the use of* The Upper Room *and* The Upper Room Disciplines. Help people with private prayer and daily reflection on scripture by promoting the use of daily devotional books available through the Upper Room. (See the "Resources" at the end of this booklet.)
- *Introduce and offer prayer for healing.* Many people have a great need for Jesus' healing touch. In special services or in the context of regular worship use the healing services in *The United Methodist Book of Worship* to offer prayer for healing to anyone who seeks it. Teach about healing using the introduction to those services.
- *Call people to a continuing conversion and renewal of the baptismal covenant.* In baptism we are called to a lifelong journey of resisting evil and trusting Christ. Advent and Lent are particular times of stirring faith toward repentance and renewal. Plan services of renewal of the baptismal covenant on the Baptism of the Lord, Easter, Pentecost, or other appropriate days. (See Baptismal Covenant I and IV in the hymnal.) If your congregation has revivals, relate the revivals to the baptismal covenant. Invite seekers into a journey toward baptism or renewal of the baptismal covenant.
- *Call seekers and newcomers to a life of faith.* Offer them opportunity to explore their questions, tell their stories, and learn the good news in Jesus Christ. Make faith sharing the work of the whole congregation. Appoint sponsors to partner with seekers. Let them mentor seekers in learning to worship, pray, reflect on scripture, and serve in daily life. Do more than make church members—pray for Christ to call disciples. *Come to the Waters* by Daniel Benedict proposes a bold model for inviting people on a conversion journey.

6. Participate in the Church Council and Charge Conference

Your church's ministry of reaching out to people, relating them to God, nurturing them in the faith, and sending them out to live as disciples in the community and world is guided by the church council. In some congregations it is called the council on ministries or the administrative council. Whatever the name, this group is a council of leaders who share a vision of the congregation's service to God in welcoming people, forming, and supporting them in a life of discipleship in daily living. You are a part of that council of spiritual leaders.

Your participation is crucial. On the one hand, you are not there merely to promote the cause of worship; you share in the concern of the leaders for the whole range of ministries aimed at making disciples and ordering the life of the congregation around the means of grace. On the other hand, the council will depend on you to be a voice of authority and passion for the centrality of worship in the congregation's life. Worship is the most distinctive and most formative action of the congregation. It is central to the flow of the church's life.

You participate to see that the whole primary task of the congregation (as illustrated in the art) is working. You lead by asking questions, envisioning how worship relates to the rest of the flow that seeks God's grace to work transforming love and justice in every person and in the whole congregation.

The charge conference is another setting for your participation and leadership. The United Methodist Church works by a series of "conferences." These conferences are understood as the settings for discerning God's will and holding the church accountable for its work in the name of God. For example, the General Conference is the worldwide conference and is responsible for the work of the whole church globally. The annual conference is a regional conference, often corresponding to the boundaries of a state. The charge conference is the local church (sometimes, several churches together) and is responsible for embodying locally Christ's ministry of making disciples. The General Conference and annual conference exist to support and resource this local ministry. The charge (local) conference reviews and evaluates the total ministry of the congregation, sets goals, and elects leaders to carry out the work. You may be asked to make a report to the meeting or to share in a group report on the ministries of the congregation.

If You Have Trouble . . .

Sometimes, there is friction in relationships. A pastor is jealous of anyone who tries to make suggestions or take initiative. A musician seems unwilling or too busy to sit down for a meeting. The congregation does not want to consider changes that would make the worship more accessible to children or to people in the neighborhood.

You can make a choice: give up or love.

- *Recognize that if you choose to love, you won't give up, and you will find an open door when it appears that all of them are closed.* If you love, you can talk to the person or persons who are resistant. Listen. See if you can see what they see, what they are afraid of.
- *Realize that you don't have to "have it your way" right now.* It isn't your way that counts as much as it is that you have a vision of something that others may not be able to see. Find out who else shares your vision. Talk with them. Find a way to share the vision with others. Discover where the resistance is. Explore ways to address that resistance.
- *Be sure the pastor is supportive of you. It is not the pastor's church, but the pastor is charged with oversight of worship.* Your job is always to work with your pastor. That is a tall order and sometimes a very difficult pathway. Walk it in love and prayer.
- *If you really get stuck, talk with the appropriate people.* If it is a staff member with whom you get stuck, talk with your pastor-parish relations committee chairperson. If it is with some leaders or members of the congregation, talk with your pastor and church council. If you need to, talk with your district superintendent and get counsel.
- *Read, go to appropriate workshops, and expand your field of view.* Maybe you will see something freshly that will open a doorway.
- *Keep loving and praying.* A lot is at stake around worship; if there are people with differing perspectives, they can become very restless and feisty. There is room at the table for all of them. You are a key leader in trying to get them to deal with diversity and to map out a way forward.

7. Discover Worship Resources

If worship is a new area of discovery and learning for you, you are in for a treat and a wonderful adventure. The books, magazines, Web sites, videos, and other resources available can be overwhelming. Don't lose heart! Take your time. Explore some basic resources. (See the resources listed at the end of this booklet.)

One good place to start is Hoyt Hickman's *United Methodist Worship*. Beyond that, be sure to spend some time reviewing *The United Methodist Book of Worship*, particularly its introductions to different sections. For example, see 13, 226, 238, 269, and 613.

8. Participate in Training Events

If you learn better in social situations, find out what training events, seminars, or workshops are available in your area. Most annual conferences and districts sponsor training opportunities related to worship. One thing you should not miss is the convocation of the Fellowship of United Methodists in Music and Worship Arts (FUMMWA). FUMMWA has a national convocation on the odd years and a jurisdictional gathering on the even-numbered years. These are wonderful opportunities for you and others (pastor, musicians, artists) to experience worship and go to workshops on a wide range of topics, especially music, dance, drama, and much more.

The Order of Saint Luke has a convocation every four years on some major worship topic, and a retreat during the other three years. These gatherings are open to any interested person.

The Institute for Worship Studies is an ecumenical organization that offers one-day "Renew Your Worship" seminars. These are excellent orientations for local church worship teams. Go to the institute's Web site, and check on dates and places nearest you. Be sure to organize so that your pastor, musician(s), and you participate together.

Review the resource list at the end of this booklet for addresses, phone numbers, and Internet addresses. Keep the list at hand.

More Paths to Vital Worship

You will want to consider other long-range possibilities. Although these are not of such central importance as those we have already discussed, it is desirable that you or some person(s) in the congregation take responsibility for them. In all these responsibilities, cooperation with the pastor is essential. *Don't worry if you are unable to do all that is suggested below. The important thing is to have your priorities clear and to know where there is a need and the readiness to move ahead.*

The Study of Worship
Encourage and enable the study of worship by individuals and groups in your congregation. Work with your pastor and other leaders to develop a plan for educating your congregation in the meaning and practices of worship. See the materials recommended for this purpose in "Resources" (pp. 29–32).

Laypersons as Worship Leaders
Our understanding of worship as the work of God's people mandates that laypersons take an active role in worship planning and leadership. Traditional roles include ushers, greeters, and acolytes, as well as the musical leaders. Laypersons increasingly are taking such worship leadership roles as reading scripture, leading prayer, witnessing, sharing concerns of the church and world, and lay speaking—not only on special occasions, such as Laity Sunday, but also every Sunday. However, they will be effective only if they are adequately trained and prepared.

Furnishings, Paraments, and Sacramental Elements
There are in every congregation furnishings, paraments, and sacramental elements for congregational worship that require ongoing attention and care. You may want to appoint persons, such as communion stewards and the altar guild, to take these responsibilities. Such persons or groups will find valuable help in the books *Worship Matters* (vol. 2) and *United Methodist Altars,* listed in "Resources" (pp. 29–32).

Multicultural Contributions
Your worship can take on new life as you enable the congregation to experience the worship style, music, art, and other contributions of various racial and ethnic groups. Doing so will not only honor and welcome persons from these cultural groups to your congregation; it will also enrich your congregation's worship experience. Multicultural resources found in *The United Methodist Hymnal, The United Methodist Book of Worship,* the Supplement to the Hymnal, and "How to Worship in Multicultural Congregations" by David Marcelo in *Worship Matters* (vol. 2) will be of value. Additional multicultural music resources are listed in "Resources."

Memorial Gifts for Worship
Many persons wish to give worship-related memorial gifts to their church, and it is important to have policies and controls to encourage needed gifts and prevent unwanted gifts. You or the worship group can take the lead in proposing a stated policy that prescribes a process for approving, placing, and using memorial gifts for worship. This is not a matter of being ungrateful; it is a matter of ensuring that items added to the "holy things" used in worship are appropriate to the environment of worship in your worship space. If you need a model for such a statement, check with some of the larger churches in your area.

Arts Other Than Music

Worship that engages all the senses will include a wider use and understanding of the arts other than music—visual, dramatic, and architectural—as expressions of faith and means of proclaiming the gospel. Possibilities include banners, vestments, paraments, chrismons, drama, interpretive movement or sacred dance, artistic bulletin covers—the possibilities are limited only by the vision and gifts of your congregation. For further information, contact the Worship Office of the General Board of Discipleship. "The Role of Artists in Worship" by Sara Webb Phillips in *Worship Matters* (vol. 1) and "The Work of Visual Artists in Worship" by Ashley Calhoun in *Worship Matters* (vol. 2) will be helpful.

Architecture is crucial for worship because the design and setup of a room will determine the character of the worship experience. As your congregation evaluates the effectiveness of its worship space and makes decisions regarding possible changes, you and other leaders of the congregation need to see that the worship space enables, rather than hinders, worship. The book *Church Architecture: Building and Renovating for Christian Worship,* listed in "Resources," is extremely valuable in guiding a congregation through such a building or renovation project.

For assistance with architecture, contact the Office of Architecture at the General Board of Global Ministries at 212-870-3868. This office offers a number of resources and services that will help you if your congregation is building or remodeling worship space.

For a resource to empower the congregation to be more sensitive and accessible to people with disabilities, secure *That All May Worship* (National Organization on Disability, 910 Sixteenth Street, NW, Suite 600, Washington DC 20006).

What About Your Church Building?

The worship space of your church makes a powerful statement. Does it say what you believe God is trying to say to the people? Or does it contradict the gospel? What do people experience? Is the message of the room a call to awe and wonder? Or is the message a call to intimacy and shared experience? Does the room invite formality or informality? How do the arrangement of symbols, play of light, acoustics, accessibility, and visibility to the actions at pulpit, font, and table shape the people's experience of God?

A Worksheet For Planning a Worship Service

Here is a planning worksheet designed for worship using the calendar of the Christian year and the Revised Common Lectionary. It can be used or adapted for other approaches to worship. You are free to adapt it for your congregation's needs. You will need one sheet for each service you are planning.

A Worksheet for Planning a Worship Service

Date: _____

Day in the church year:
_____

Planning team:
_____
_____

Liturgical color: _____

Scripture readings:
  First reading: _____
  Psalm response: _____
  Second reading: _____

Will there be Communion? _____
  Baptism? _____

Special emphasis or special service?
_____

Gospel reading: _____

Sermon focus: _____
_____

Hymns/songs:
_____
_____
_____
_____
_____
_____

Anthems:
_____
_____

Service/communion music:
_____
_____

Instrumental music:
_____

Assisting ministers/readers:
_____
_____

Acolytes: _____
_____

Other participants (actors, dancers, technicians, instrumentalists):
_____
_____
_____

Visuals: _____
_____

Invitations to be made (commitment to discipleship, healing prayer):
_____

Other details for this service:
_____
_____
_____

Evaluation/Improvement:
• What worked well?
• What could be improved?
• In what ways? What did we learn?
• How will our learning be incorporated into next week's service?

Resources

Addresses and Phone Numbers
For further assistance, contact:
The Worship Resourcing Team
General Board of Discipleship
P.O. Box 340003, Nashville, TN 37202-0003
Telephone: toll-free 877-899-2780 or toll 615-340-7070
Fax: 615-340-7015

The following will give you more direct access to specific help in several areas of worship:

- For a huge amount of help in the area of worship, visit the Worship Web site: http://www.gbod.org/worship/default.html.
- For information on music in churches with small membership, call 877-899-2780, extension 7073.
- For ideas on welcoming seekers and making disciples through worship, call 877-899-2780, extension 7072.
- For resources related to preaching, call 877-899-2780, extension 7053.
- Discipleship Resources, P.O. Box 34003, Nashville, TN 37202-0003. For ordering, call 800-685-4370. For information about resources and help with selections, call 800-814-7833, or fax 770-442-5114.
  Web site: http://www.discipleshipresources.com.
- Cokesbury Service Center, 800-672-1789, for items marked "available from Cokesbury." Cokesbury Online is http://www.cokesbury.com.
- The Upper Room, P.O. Box 189, Nashville, TN 37202-0189. For information and ordering, call 800-972-0433. Web site: http://www.upperroom.org. The Upper Room offers a full line of resources for spiritual formation and guidance.
- Curric-U-Phone, 800-251-8591, for church school publications.
  EcuFilm, 800-251-4091, for video and film resources.
- Office of Architecture, the General Board of Global Ministries.
  Call 212-870-3868 or contact rpatterson@gbgm-umc.org. This office offers a number of resources and services that will help your congregation with building planning processes for new structures or renovation.

General Church Print Resources
Those marked with an asterisk (*) are especially useful for your work with worship.
The Book of Discipline of The United Methodist Church, 2000
(Cokesbury, 800-672-1789).
The Interpreter (United Methodist Communications, 615-742-5110). The official program journal for United Methodist leaders. Issued eight times a year. Seven copies provided free to church officers selected by the pastor.
**Program Calendar* (United Methodist Communications, 615-742-5110). A helpful tool for planning worship in the context of the larger programs and ministries of the church. Lectionary readings are listed for each Sunday and special day.

Basic Worship Planning Resources

The Acolyte's Book, by Hoyt L. Hickman (Cokesbury, 800-672-1789). A training book for use by acolytes.

*Blended Worship, by Robert E. Webber. Offers detailed and practical guidance on achieving substance and relevance in worship. For churches that want to blend contemporary music and approaches with the core of the Christian worship tradition, this is a very useful resource.

*By Water and the Spirit: Making Connections for Identity and Ministry, by Gayle C. Felton (available from Discipleship Resources). Contains the official paper on baptism adopted by General Conference in 1996 with a study commentary and guidance for leading a group study of six sessions.

Children Worship (Discipleship Resources, 800-685-4370). A complete resource for local church leaders, pastors, and congregations aimed at welcoming children and their gifts in worship.

Church Architecture: Building and Renovating for Christian Worship, by James F. White and Susan White (Cokesbury, 800-672-1789, or Order of Saint Luke Publications, 330-434-0110).

Come to the Waters, by Daniel Benedict (Discipleship Resources, 800-685-4370). This book looks at baptism and the congregation's ministry of welcoming seekers and making Christian disciples.

*Contemporary Worship for the 21st Century: Worship or Evangelism?, by Daniel Benedict and Craig Kennet Miller (available from Discipleship Resources). A resource for congregations seeking to expand the range of worship options within existing worship settings or in adding worship services.

Helping Youth Pray (Cokesbury, 800-672-1789). One of twelve small booklets in the Skillabilities for Youth Ministry series.

*Mil Voces Para Celebrar (Cokesbury, 800-672-1789). The official Spanish language hymnal and worship book.

That All May Worship (National Organization on Disability, 910 Sixteenth Street, NW, Suite 600, Washington, DC 20006; 202-293-5960). A basic resource that empowers the congregation to be sensitive to people with disabilities and to make worship space accessible to them.

*United Methodist Altars, by Hoyt L. Hickman (Cokesbury, 800-672-1789). A manual for all who do the work of altar guilds and a resource for pastors and worship chairpersons.

*The United Methodist Book of Worship (Cokesbury, 800-672-1789). The official book of worship, revised in 1992, for planners and leaders of worship. Lectionary on pp. 227-37. This volume has resources for worship throughout the Christian year and for observances of special days.

*The United Methodist Hymnal: Book of United Methodist Worship (Cokesbury, 800-672-1789). Our official hymn and worship book. Contains official United Methodist general services: baptism, Holy Communion, marriage, funeral.

*The United Methodist Music and Worship Planner is published annually with lectionary readings printed in full text, suggested colors, hymns, anthems, contemporary and instrumental music.

*United Methodist Worship, by Hoyt L. Hickman (Cokesbury, 800-672-1789). An

introduction to United Methodist worship for personal or group study.
The United Methodist Worship Planning Calendar (Cokesbury, 800-672-1789). Published annually with lectionary readings, suggested colors, hymn suggestions, and planning space for each Sunday. Lectionary readings for each Sunday are listed.
Worship and Daily Life (Discipleship Resources, 800-685-4370). Offers prayers, litanies, calls to worship, and more that focus on the ministry of Christians in daily life. It contains a useful guide for selecting hymns for affirming the daily life ministry.
Worship Blueprints, by Andy Langford (Cokesbury, 800-672-1789). A basic book on how to design worship services, complete with work sheets, based on The United Methodist Hymnal and The United Methodist Book of Worship.
Worship Matters: A United Methodist Guide to Ways of Worship, vol. 1, edited by E. Byron Anderson, and *Worship Matters: A United Methodist Guide to Worship Work,* vol. 2, edited by E. Byron Anderson (Discipleship Resources, 800-685-4370). Every local church should have these basic volumes. They give basic perspectives on worship in our tradition and help with practical issues for strengthening worship.
The Worship Resources of The United Methodist Hymnal, edited by Hoyt Hickman (Cokesbury, 800-672-1789). This book helps pastors, musicians, and other leaders of worship understand and use *The United Methodist Hymnal.*

Music Resources

(See *The United Methodist Hymnal* and *The United Methodist Book of Worship* above.) Unless otherwise noted, all of these are available from Cokesbury, 800-672-1789.
Changing Your Tune, Lynn Hurst. Guides worship leaders through various aspects necessary for meaningful leadership in contemporary services.
Expanded Edition Cokesbury Chorus Book, edited by Andy Langford, contains popular contemporary praise and worship choruses for worship.
Companion to the United Methodist Hymnal, edited by Carlton Young, offers background on every hymn tune and text in *The United Methodist Hymnal* as well as information regarding music in The United Methodist Church.
Hymns from the Four Winds. A collection of Asian-American hymns.
The Hymns of The United Methodist Hymnal, edited by Diana Sanchez. This book helps pastors, musicians, and other leaders of worship to appreciate and use the hymns in the hymnal and to discover fresh ways to sing and accompany them.
Praise Now! Ready-to-Use Services for Contemporary Worship, Lynn Hurst and Sherrell Boles. Suggestions for complete services, including sermon ideas, drama, music, and visual suggestions.
Songs of Zion. A songbook from the African-American religious tradition
The United Methodist Book of Worship Accompaniment Edition. Offers worship leaders and musicians full score for the "Music as Acts of Worship" section of the *Book of Worship.*
The United Methodist Music and Worship Planner is published annually with lectionary readings printed in full text, suggested colors, hymns, anthems, contemporary and instrumental music.
The Faith We Sing (supplement to *The United Methodist Hymnal*) contains a sig-

nificant collection of new hymns, songs for praise and worship, global music, old favorites for expanding the range of congregational song. Available in several editions: pew, accompaniment, simplified, singers, worship planner, guitar, audio, CD-ROM, and MIDI. Available in late 2000.
The United Methodist Choir Director's Organizer (annual), Ginger G. Wyrick. Includes a United Methodist Hymnal usage chart, calendar noting special days, and more reproducible forms and worksheets September through August.

Preaching Resources
Freedom in the Pulpit: A Vision for Growth in Preaching, by Barbara Bate (Discipleship Resources, 800-685-4370).

Catalogs
The Cokesbury Catalog: United Methodist Edition. A comprehensive catalog of resources for the local church. Free. Call 800-672-1789.
Cokesbury Music Catalogs: (Comprehensive Catalog of Resources for Music Ministry. Call 877-877-8674.
Discipleship Resources Comprehensive Catalog. A free catalog of resources, including worship resources, for local churches (available through Discipleship Resources, P.O. Box 189, Nashville, TN 37202-0189).
Web site: http://www.discipleshipresources.org.
Upper Room Catalog. A free catalog of worship and devotional resources (available through the Upper Room, P.O. Box 189, Nashville, TN 37202-0189).
Web site: http://www.upperroom.org.

Organizations
The Fellowship of United Methodists in Music and Worship Arts, P.O. Box 24787, Nashville, TN 37202-4787. Call 800-952-8977, or toll 615-749-6875.
Fax: 615-340-7006. E-mail: FUMMWA@aol.com. Web site:
http://members.aol.com/fummwa/fummwa.htm. The fellowship is a membership organization providing resources and support for music and the arts in worship. The journal, *Worship Arts,* is published bimonthly. Membership includes professional and nonprofessional musicians, clergy, and persons interested in worship and the arts.

The Order of Saint Luke, P.O. Box 22279, Akron, OH 44302-0079. Telephone and fax: 330-535-8656. Web site: http://www.Saint-Luke.org. This is a community of people devoted to sacramental and liturgical scholarship, education, and practice. The order includes laypersons, seminarians, and clergy. It publishes *Sacramental Life and Doxology.* The order holds a retreat each year that is open to anyone interested in the retreat's theme.

Cokesbury Music Service, call 877-877-8674. Fax: 800-445-8189. Internet: www.cokesburymusic.com. Music service that allows ordering resources from most music publishers on one account.